INTRO TO PHYSICS Need to Know

SilverTip

Gravity

by Karen Latchana Kenney

Consultant: Kathy Renfrew
Science Educator and Science Learner

BEARPORT
PUBLISHING

Minneapolis, Minnesota

Credits

Cover and title page, © limpido/Shutterstock; 4–5, © BDLook/Shutterstock; 6–7, © Siri Stafford/iStock; 9T, © Vladimir Melnikov/Shutterstock; 9C, © Gorodenkoff/Shutterstock; 9B, © Evgeny555/iStock; 12–13, © dima_zel/iStock; 15, © Aaron Foster/Getty Images; 18–19, © irabell/iStock; 20–21, © adventtr/iStock; 22, © Hakase_/iStock; 23, © EreborMountain/Shutterstock; 25, © NASA/JPL-Caltech, IPAC/Jet Propulsion Laboratory; and 27, © IvaFoto/Shutterstock.

Bearport Publishing Company Product Development Team

President: Jen Jenson; Director of Product Development: Spencer Brinker; Senior Editor: Allison Juda; Editor: Charly Haley; Associate Editor: Naomi Reich; Senior Designer: Colin O'Dea; Associate Designer: Elena Klinkner; Product Development Assistant: Anita Stasson

Library of Congress Cataloging-in-Publication Data is available at www.loc.gov or upon request from the publisher.

ISBN: 979-8-88509-221-0 (hardcover)
ISBN: 979-8-88509-228-9 (paperback)
ISBN: 979-8-88509-235-7 (ebook)

Copyright © 2023 Bearport Publishing Company. All rights reserved. No part of this publication may be reproduced in whole or in part, stored in any retrieval system, or transmitted in any form or by any means, electronic, mechanical, photocopying, recording, or otherwise, without written permission from the publisher.

For more information, write to Bearport Publishing, 5357 Penn Avenue South, Minneapolis, MN 55419. Printed in the United States of America.

Contents

A Big Pull. 4
Use the Forces. 6
Gravity Matters. 10
Gravity on Earth 14
A Moving Moon 16
The Strong Sun 20
Galaxies and Beyond 24
A Mysterious Force 26

Gravity's Strength 28
SilverTips for Success 29
Glossary .30
Read More 31
Learn More Online 31
Index 32
About the Author 32

A Big Pull

Skateboarding downhill takes some serious skill. You start out slow. But as you make your way down, you pick up speed. It's tricky to stay on your board as you zoom faster and faster. What pulls you down the hill so fast? It's gravity.

Scientist Isaac Newton was the first person to write about gravity. He described it in his 1687 book about motion.

Use the Forces

Gravity is a kind of **force**. These are the pushes and pulls that effect how objects move.

Some forces are at work when two objects touch. You kick a soccer ball, and the force pushes the ball along. But other forces aren't as easy to see with just your eye.

Forces between two objects that touch are called contact forces. There are many of these forces. Some push objects along. Others pull objects or make them stop.

Some forces work without touching. Gravity pulls large objects toward one another. Its pull sends a dropped book speeding toward the floor. Gravity keeps people and buildings on Earth. And it also pulls on the moon to keep it circling our planet.

Unlike many forces, gravity works over long distances. **Magnetism** is another force that can work without two objects touching.

Gravity Matters

What can gravity pull? Everything with **matter**! This includes anything you can see or touch.

The *amount* of matter also matters. We measure matter in **mass**, or by how much stuff is in something. The more mass something has, the stronger its pull of gravity.

> Matter on Earth can be in three main forms, or states. They are solid, liquid, and gas. Some matter can change from one state to another. Liquid water changes to solid ice or gassy steam as temperatures change.

An elephant has much more mass than a mouse.

All things with mass pull on all other things with mass. But some pull more strongly. People don't have much mass, so their gravity isn't very strong. On the other hand, a planet has lots of matter. Earth's gravity keeps soil, plants, and animals all stuck to its surface.

Rocket engines have to work hard to escape Earth's gravity. They burn fuel to push a rocket into space. This force pushing away from the planet has to be stronger than gravity's pull toward Earth.

Gravity on Earth

Gravity also helps make Earth livable. In addition to pulling on things we see, it also pulls gases toward the planet. These gases form a blanket around Earth called the **atmosphere**. This protects the planet from dangerous things in space. It also holds the air we breathe.

> The atmosphere keeps water on Earth, too. It traps water in clouds around the planet. Then, gravity pulls the water back down to the ground as rain.

A Moving Moon

Earth's gravity reaches far into space. It keeps the moon circling the planet in a path called an orbit. The moon keeps moving forward through space. At the same time, gravity pulls the moon toward Earth. These two motions keep the moon in orbit.

> Imagine the moon like a cannon fired from the top of a mountain that pokes into space. The firing force combines with gravity to create a path that is a circle around the planet.

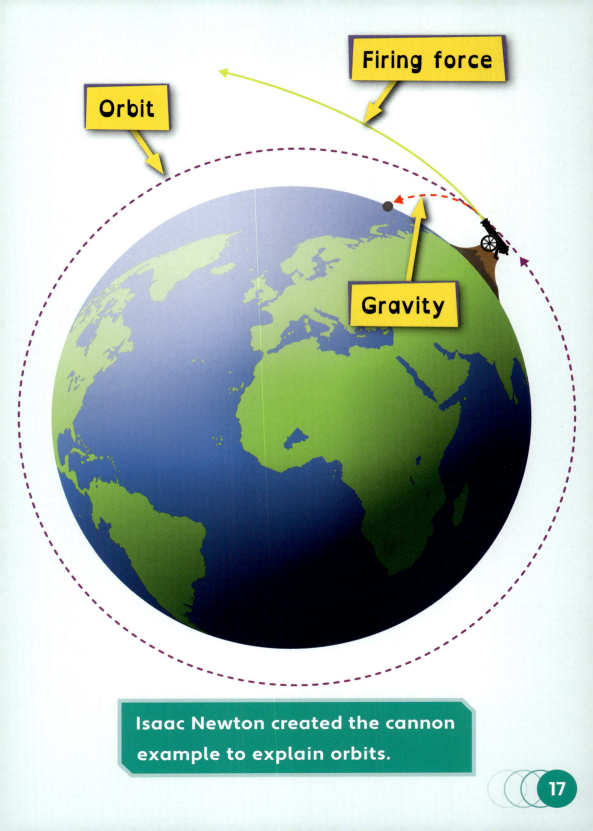

Isaac Newton created the cannon example to explain orbits.

Gravity between objects goes both ways. Gravity from the moon pulls on Earth, too. Because of its smaller mass, the moon's gravity is much weaker. Still, its pull does have an effect. It makes ocean water bulge out from the planet.

The moon's pull on water creates **tides**. Areas that are farther from the moon have low tides. Places where the moon is closer have high tides. Tides change as the moon moves around Earth.

The Strong Sun

Beyond Earth and the moon, something even bigger holds onto us. The sun's mass is more than 300,000 times greater than Earth's. Its gravity is very strong. Just as Earth pulls the moon, the sun pulls to keep Earth, other planets, and space objects in orbit.

Eight planets orbit our sun. The sun's gravity also affects more than 200 moons, comets, and asteroids.

Like all planets, Earth doesn't travel in a perfect circle around the sun. This has to do with gravity, too. The sun's gravity is stronger when a planet is closer. Then, it speeds the planet's movement. It slows a planet down when it gets farther away. This stretches the orbit into an oval.

Imagine speed in a planet's orbit like someone on a swing. The person speeds up as they are pulled toward Earth. They slow as they get farther from the ground. Eventually, Earth's gravity pulls them back again.

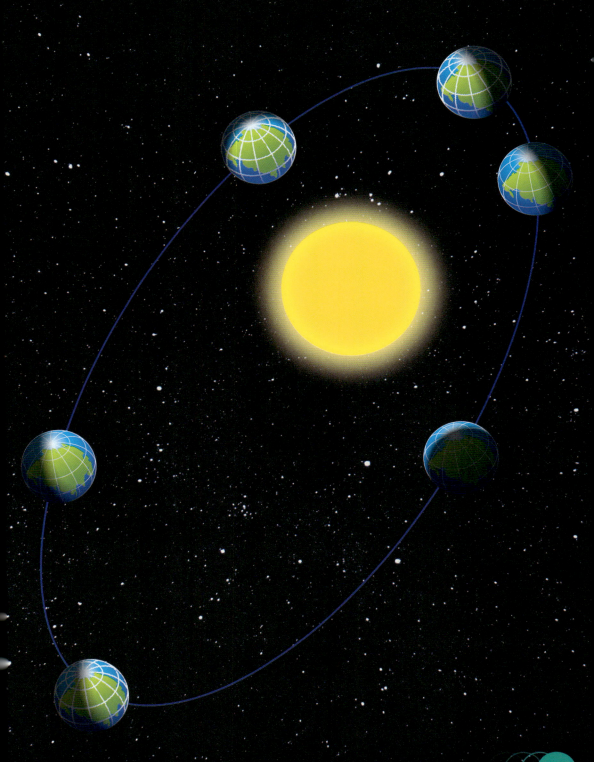

Galaxies and Beyond

Our sun and the planets in orbit around it are only a small part of the larger Milky Way **galaxy**. The galaxy's gravity pulls together more than 100 billion stars and many hundreds of billions of planets. Each galaxy's gravity also affects other galaxies.

> Scientists think each galaxy has a center where gravity is even stronger. These places are packed with a lot of mass in a very small space. Scientists call them black holes.

The strong gravity of black holes pulls in everything. This includes light.

A Mysterious Force

Gravity still holds many mysteries. We see its effects on large objects, such as planets. But scientists do not completely understand how it works in dark, distant space. They study gravity's force on tiny objects, too. Their work may help us better understand the force that holds the universe together.

> Space telescopes let us look farther in our galaxy and beyond. The James Webb telescope launched in December 2021. It helps scientists learn more about gravity in the Milky Way galaxy.

Gravity's Strength

Gravity acts on all objects with mass. But the force is stronger at some times than at others.

Gravity's force depends on mass.

The force is smaller for objects with less mass.

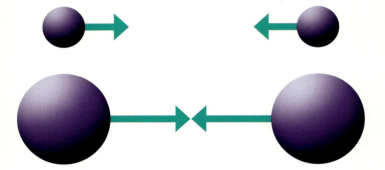

Gravity's force depends on distance.

Gravity gets weaker as the distance between objects grows.

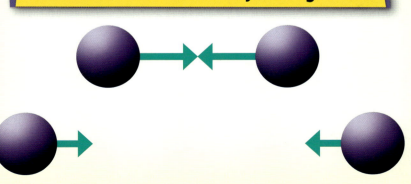

SilverTips for SUCCESS

⭐ SilverTips for REVIEW

Review what you've learned. Use the text to help you.

Define key terms

force matter
galaxy orbit
mass

Check for understanding

How are mass and gravity related?

What does Earth's gravity do to objects on the planet? What does it do to objects beyond the planet?

Describe how gravity keeps objects in orbit.

Think deeper

What do you think might happen if the pull of Earth's gravity was weaker?

⭐ SilverTips on TEST-TAKING

- **Make a study plan.** Ask your teacher what the test is going to cover. Then, set aside time to study a little bit every day.

- **Read all the questions carefully.** Be sure you know what is being asked.

- **Skip any questions** you don't know how to answer right away. Mark them and come back later if you have time.

Glossary

atmosphere a layer of gases that surrounds a planet

force a push or a pull that causes movement

galaxy a large group of planets and stars

magnetism a force produced by a magnet that attracts metal objects to the magnet

mass a measure of the amount or quantity of something

matter the material that makes up all objects

orbit the path of an object that is circling a planet or the sun

tides the movement of water toward or away from the shore

Read More

Enz, Tammy. *Forces at the Amusement Park (Amusement Park Science).* North Mankato, MN: Capstone, 2020.

Faust, Daniel R. *Gravitational, Magnetic, & Electric Forces: Examining Interactions (Spotlight on Physical Science).* New York: PowerKids Press, 2020.

Finan, Catherine C. *Planets and Moons (X-Treme Facts: Space).* Minneapolis: Bearport Publishing, 2022.

Learn More Online

1. Go to **www.factsurfer.com** or scan the QR code below.
2. Enter "**Physics Gravity**" into the search box.
3. Click on the cover of this book to see a list of websites.

Index

atmosphere 14–15

cannon 16–17

forces 6, 8, 12, 16–17, 26, 28

galaxy 24, 26

life 12

mass 10–12, 18, 20, 24, 28

matter 10, 12

moon 8, 16, 18, 20

Newton, Isaac 4, 17

orbits 16–17, 20, 22, 24

planets 12, 20, 22, 24, 26

sun 20, 22, 24

tides 18

About the Author

Karen Latchana Kenney is an author from Minnesota. She was born by the equator, where gravity is weaker on Earth's surface.